Bake Your Own
SODA BREAD

BY MARI BOLTE

PEBBLE
a capstone imprint

Published by Pebble, an imprint of Capstone
1710 Roe Crest Drive, North Mankato, Minnesota 56003
capstonepub.com

Copyright © 2026 by Capstone. All rights reserved. No part of this publication may be reproduced in whole or in part, or stored in a retrieval system, or transmitted in any form or by any means, electronic, mechanical, photocopying, recording, or otherwise, without written permission of the publisher.

Library of Congress Cataloging-in-Publication Data
Names: Bolte, Mari, author.
Title: Bake your own soda bread / by Mari Bolte.
Description: North Mankato, Minnesota : Pebble, an imprint of Capstone, [2026] | Series: Pebble maker baking | Audience: Ages 5–8 | Audience: Grades 2–3 | Summary: "Fresh bread is yummy to smell and even tastier to eat! Early and emergent readers can bake their own loaf of soft soda bread topped with honey butter. Step-by-step instructions plus clear photos guide elementary children through this simple recipe that they (with a little adult assistance) can make themselves—and then enjoy!"— Provided by publisher.
Identifiers: LCCN 2024052317 (print) | LCCN 2024052318 (ebook) | ISBN 9798875224461 (hardcover) | ISBN 9798875224416 (paperback) | ISBN 9798875224423 (pdf) | ISBN 9798875224430 (epub) | ISBN 9798875224447 (kindle edition)
Subjects: LCSH: Bread—Juvenile literature. | LCGFT: Cookbooks.
Classification: LCC TX769 .B60155 2026 (print) | LCC TX769 (ebook) | DDC 641.81/5—dc23/eng/20241205
LC record available at https://lccn.loc.gov/2024052317
LC ebook record available at https://lccn.loc.gov/2024052318

Editorial Credits
Editor: Abby Cich; Designer: Heidi Thompson; Media Researcher: Jo Miller; Production Specialist: Tori Abraham

Image Credits
Capstone: Karen Dubke, front and back cover, 1, 8, 9, 11–13, 15, 17–21; Shutterstock: Prostock-studio, 7, RoJo Images, 23, Tracy Morgan, 5

The publisher and the author shall not be liable for any damages allegedly arising from the information in this book, and they specifically disclaim any liability from the use or application of any of the contents of this book.

Any additional websites and resources referenced in this book are not maintained, authorized, or sponsored by Capstone. All product and company names are trademarks™ or registered® trademarks of their respective holders.

Printed and bound in China. 6274

TABLE OF CONTENTS

Bread and Butter 4

Kitchen Tips 6

What You Need 8

What You Do 10

Take It Further 22

Glossary 24

About the Author 24

Words in **BOLD** are in the glossary.

BREAD AND BUTTER

People have been making bread for more than 10,000 years. Today, it is one of the world's most popular foods. Some breads use **yeast** to **rise**. Soda bread does not. Buttermilk and baking soda make it fluffy.

Get baking! A slice of soda bread with honey butter is waiting for you!

KITCHEN TIPS

Stay safe and have fun with these tips.

- Have an adult helper nearby. Ask them to help with hot or sharp things.

- Read the recipe before you start. Get all your **ingredients** and tools.

- Wash your hands before you begin.

- Help clean up when you are done!

WHAT YOU NEED

TOOLS

- 9-inch (23-centimeter) square baking pan or pie plate
- cooking spray
- measuring cups and spoons
- large mixing bowl and spoon
- fork
- **cooling rack**
- small bowl
- spoon or spatula

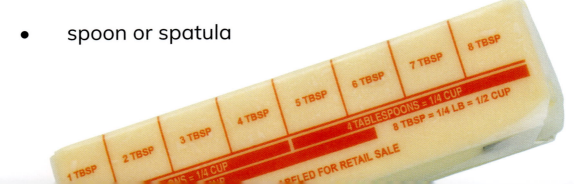

INGREDIENTS FOR THE BREAD

- 2 1/4 cups (270 grams) flour
- 1/2 teaspoon (3 g) baking soda
- 1/2 teaspoon (3 g) salt
- 1 tablespoon (12 g) white sugar
- 1 cup (240 milliliters) buttermilk, cold

INGREDIENTS FOR THE HONEY BUTTER

- 1/2 cup (113 g) salted butter, room temperature
- 1/4 cup (59 mL) honey
- 1/2 teaspoon (5 mL) vanilla **extract**

WHAT YOU DO

STEP 1

Spray the inside of the baking pan with cooking spray. Ask an adult to **preheat** the oven to 450°F (232°C).

STEP 2

Put the flour and baking soda in the large bowl. Add the salt and sugar too. Stir it all together.

Make a wide hole in the middle of the flour **mixture**. Pour the buttermilk into the hole. Use a fork to slowly stir the flour into the milk. The **dough** will be thick and sticky!

STEP 3

Sprinkle extra flour on a clean work surface. Then scrape the dough onto it.

Add some flour to your hands. With your hands, lift one side of the dough. Fold it gently to the center. Fold another side. Fold a few more times. Go until the dough is a circle about 6 inches (15.2 cm) wide.

STEP 4

Set the dough in the pan. Ask the adult to make an X-shape in the middle with a knife.

STEP 5

Bake the bread for 10 minutes. Then, have the adult lower the oven to 400°F (200°C). Bake for 20 minutes more. Is the bread golden brown? It is done!

Let the bread cool in the pan for 10 minutes. Then take the bread out. Set it on the cooling rack. Cool for at least 30 minutes.

STEP 6

While the bread cools, make honey butter! Put the butter in the small bowl. Add the honey and vanilla. Stir it all up with a spoon or spatula. Enjoy it on a slice of soda bread!

Store extra bread in a dish with a lid. It will stay fresh for three days. Keep the butter in the fridge. Eat it within one month.

TAKE IT FURTHER

Add fruit to your bread! Stir in 1/2 cup (74 g) raisins to the flour mixture.

Make things sweet. Add 1/4 teaspoon (1 g) cinnamon to the flour. Put in an extra tablespoon (12 g) of sugar too.

With an adult, use extra bread to make French toast. Or make a tasty grilled cheese!

GLOSSARY

cooling rack (KOO-ling RAK)—a wire rack that helps to cool a baked good by allowing air to flow under it

dough (DOH)—a mixture of flour and water or other food (such as yeast, fat, or sugar) that is ready to be baked

extract (EK-strakt)—a liquid used for flavoring food

ingredient (in-GREE-dee-uhnt)—a food that is put with other foods to make a recipe

mixture (MIKS-cher)—two or more ingredients that have been mixed together

preheat (PREE-heet)—to heat an oven to a certain temperature before baking

rise (RAHYZ)—when dough expands due to carbon dioxide gas; yeast produces carbon dioxide, but so does mixing buttermilk and baking soda

yeast (YEEST)—a microscopic fungus used in baking that turns sugar into carbon dioxide

ABOUT THE AUTHOR

Mari Bolte has been baking—and writing books about baking—since the beginning of time. (Well, it feels like that, anyway.) These days, she squeezes in loaves of no-knead bread and trays of sweet treats in between writing projects.